D0831615

The People
vs.
Judas Iscariot

... the punishment phase

Worship And Drama Series
For Lent

Wm. Clayton McCord

CSS Publishing Company, Inc., Lima, Ohio

THE PEOPLE VS. JUDAS ISCARIOT
... the punishment phase

Copyright © 1999 by
CSS Publishing Company, Inc.
Lima, Ohio

Scripture quotations are from the *Revised Standard Version of the Bible*, copyrighted 1946, 1952 ©, 1971, 1973, by the Division of Christian Education of the National Council of the Churches of Christ in the USA. Used by permission.

Scripture quotations marked NRSV are from the *New Revised Standard Version of the Bible*, copyright 1989 by the Division of Christian Education of the National Council of the Churches of Christ in the USA. Used by permission.

Library of Congress Cataloging-in-Publication Data

McCord, Wm. Clayton (William Clayton), 1957-
   The people vs. Judas Iscariot : the punishment phase / Wm. Clayton McCord.
     p.   cm.
   "Worship and drama series for Lent."
   ISBN 0-7880-1311-4 (pbk.)
   1. Judas Iscariot—Drama. 2. Bible. N.T.—History of Biblical events—Drama.
I. Title. II. Title: People versus Judas Iscariot.
PS3563.C344382P46   1999
812'.54—dc21   98-47230
                                                 CIP

ISBN 0-7880-1311-4
PRINTED IN U.S.A.

To my wife Patricia,
whose grace comes freely and undeserved,

and to my mother Helen,
who always believed
there was a writer in me.

Table Of Contents

Foreword   7

Author's Preface   9

Goals And Objectives   13

Scenario   15

Setting   19

Lenten Series:

The Prosecution's Case
Lent 1
   Sample Bulletin   21
   Act 1 — Nothing Is Hidden From God   23

Lent 2
   Sample Bulletin   35
   Act II — All Have Sinned — All Need Forgiveness   37

Lent 3
   Sample Bulletin   51
   Act III — When Others Tried To Save Themselves   53

The Defense's Case
Lent 4
   Sample Bulletin   73
   Act IV — In Bondage To Sin:We Cannot Free Ourselves   75

Lent 5
   Sample Bulletin   93
   Act V — Who Will Save Us?   95

Foreword

Clay conceived the idea for this book some years ago while still a seminarian in the Lutheran Program at Austin, Texas. In homiletics class we were discussing the problematic of following the rules of rhetoric, keeping a balance between the principles of law and gospel, having all parts serve a clear theme and at one and the same time being faithful to scripture and tradition without stifling creativity.

In attempting to demonstrate various possibilities for shaping sermons, Clay opined that for him chancel drama might be a perfect medium in which he could pull all these factors together. It was then and there that he said he thought he would put Judas on trial and I responded that I would like to see him do it.

Because of the way life is for seminarians and beginning pastors, the idea was put on the back burner for some time. Finally, though long in gestation, the idea was given birth and the product is beautiful to behold. It is not only well done for communication to the congregation, it is thoughtfully formatted for the busy pastor who will appreciate its summary overview, its carefully selected scripture readings, and even fully detailed service bulletins for the five weeks of Lent apart from Holy Week. Here you have it, a masterful blending of gospel proclamation with powerful drama. It is effective gospel preaching without ever becoming preachy.

H. C. Krause
Professor Emeritus of Homiletic and Hispanic Ministry
Wartburg Theological Seminary and
Episcopal Theological Seminary of the Southwest

Author's Preface

I have always wondered about the eternal fate of Judas Iscariot, the betrayer of Jesus. Was he beyond forgiveness? How is our sinfulness different?

The story of his betrayal and confession holds in tension the judgment of God on the one hand and the free grace of God on the other. In this tension I saw a connection to the theme of Lent: an honest accounting of our own guilt and need for salvation and renewal. The result was *The People vs. Judas Iscariot*, a five-part series for Lenten worship or group discussion.

I wanted a series that would honor the theme of Lent and beckon introspection. I wanted to keep it Christ-centered. And I wanted a series that involved very little preparation by the pastor or participants.

The goal of *The People vs. Judas Iscariot* is based upon the Ash Wednesday reading of Joel 2:13: "Return to the Lord, your God, for God is gracious and merciful; slow to anger and abounding in steadfast love...." The series is guided by three objectives: 1) to revisit the passion narrative, hearing details through key witnesses in ways we might not have considered before now; 2) to prompt reflection upon our own need for forgiveness; and 3) to focus on the sacrificial death of Jesus Christ and his suffering for the sins of the world.

In this series Judas undergoes the punishment phase of his trial. He has already plead guilty to a crime against Jesus. Now the question is: "Is anything serious enough to merit God's abandonment?" Does Judas receive mercy or eternal punishment?

Each Act (or homily) unfolds in the middle of worship, taking the shape of a modern-day courtroom drama in which prosecution and defense attorneys attempt to sway the judge and congregation with evidence based upon scripture and tradition. Different witnesses are subpoenaed to testify, including Peter, John, the Unnamed Woman, Mary Magdalene, the Chief Priest, and others. Their testimony transports us back in time to the events that surrounded Jesus' betrayal and crucifixion. When I completed this series for my own church, I actually polled the congregation for a verdict. The results were interesting, to say the least.

It is important to note that we do not presume to hold our decision above God's decision. The purpose is to reflect on the justice of God's law — exposing our sin — and the extent of God's Grace through faith in Jesus Christ, by struggling with the case of *The People vs. Judas Iscariot*.

You will find this series easy to present. Included are five worship outlines and scripture readings that follow closely guarded themes. The worship leader needs only to choose the hymns.

The nave and sanctuary are transformed effortlessly into a courtroom setting (*refer to "Setting" in this book*). Since lawyers work from notes and judges have books on their bench, I found that participants could easily work "cold" with scripts in front of them. Absolutely no memorization required! Witnesses testify from the lectern with their scripts in front of them. When I produced this series for my church, the congregation had no idea that it was unrehearsed.

I did not bother with costumes, either. The congregation seemed to accept the witnesses of the past in modern attire — since they were witnesses summoned into a modern-day court. The only exception was the character "Death," who wore a Grim Reaper costume and whose face was hidden from view.

The People vs. Judas Iscariot also lends itself to discussion groups during Lent. Sunday School teachers (junior high through adult) might use this book as a creative tool for their classes. Or the series may be used as a drama presentation by youth groups. Because this book is somewhat provocative in its arguments on both sides, it lends itself extremely well to discussion groups as well as presentations.

I want to thank those who helped make this series possible, especially my wife Pat, with her legal expertise and patience; Gary Smith, from the Law Offices of Gary W. Smith, who made editorial changes to the trial's "objections and rebuttals"; Melissa Morgan, Art Masters, Jason Ramm, Linda Mitchell, Nathan Bruhn, Anna and Chuck Griffiths, Marvin Eargle, Brandon Callies, Janet

Fisher, Geoffrey Royall, Mark Wright, and Gretchen Combs, whose insights and support brought this series to life; and Hilmer Krause, to whom I am indebted for the inspiration to write this book.

Reverend Wm. Clayton McCord
Redeemer Lutheran Church
Greenville, Texas

Goals And Objectves

Goals:
A. **Guiding Scripture:** *"Return to the Lord, your God, for God is gracious and merciful; slow to anger and abounding in steadfast love...."* Joel 2:13, Ash Wednesday Lesson
B. **Focus** on the suffering and sacrificial death of Jesus Christ
C. **Reflect** on our own need for forgiveness
D. **Revisit** the passion narrative as told through key witnesses in court

Objectives:

Series:	Courtroom Drama (five parts), depicting the punishment phase of Judas Iscariot
Worship:	Drama becomes the homily, unfolding at the heart of each worship service
Setting:	Modern-day courtroom; witnesses are summoned from the past
Jury:	Congregation
Prosecutor:	Justice, representing the Law of God which convicts us of our sins
Defense:	Grace, representing the Grace of God which saves us
Witnesses:	*For the Prosecution:* Disciple John, Mary Magdalene, Unnamed Woman, Disciple Peter, the Young Boy, Mary (mother of Jesus) *For the Defense:* Friend of Judas, Chief Priest, Apostle Paul, Death (personified)
Acts:	Five; one for each week during Lent
Themes:	Five; one for each act; overall thematic movement leads us from conviction of our sins toward Good Friday and the Cross
Sample Bulletins:	Five worship outlines with confessions and scriptures to support weekly themes

Scenario

Act I
Theme: Nothing Is Hidden From God

Congregation is "sworn in" as jury. *JUDGE* addresses congregation, outlining their duty to determine the punishment of *JUDAS*. Within that context, *JUDGE* states that we are *not* attempting to hold our judgment above God's judgment; rather, the congregation is to "prayerfully consider" the justice of God's law which exposes our sin, and the extent of God's grace through faith in Jesus Christ which saves us — the theme of Lent. Prosecution attorney *JUSTICE* and defense attorney *GRACE* address their opening statements.

The prosecution then begins its case with the testimony of the disciple *JOHN*. Through *JOHN's* testimony, the prosecution attempts to verify that Jesus knew *JUDAS* was "evil" and "unclean" from the very beginning. Under cross-examination by the defense, *JOHN* reveals that he, too, was a sinner; he was once known as "Son of Thunder" for his temper, and he had desires for glory to be at the right side of Jesus in the kingdom. That nothing is hidden from God convicts us all. Court is recessed.

Act II
Theme: All Have Sinned — All Need Forgiveness

Prosecution attorney *JUSTICE* calls the next witness, *MARY MAGDALENE*, who gives further damaging testimony about the character of *JUDAS*. When asked if she ever heard *JUDAS* ask for forgiveness, she says no — nor did she ever hear Jesus forgive him. Defense attorney *GRACE* challenges *MARY MAGDALENE's* testimony, forcing her to admit that all people are sinners and all need forgiveness; most importantly, that Jesus said from the cross, "Father, forgive them for they know not what they do."

Following *MARY MAGDALENE's* fiery cross-examination under the defense, *JUSTICE* calls the next witness, the *UNNAMED WOMAN*, revealed to be Mary of Bethany. She retells how she

15

anointed Jesus prior to his crucifixion; how *JUDAS* objected to the act, then left the house to betray Jesus.

Just as the defense seeks to show that *JUDAS* was not the only one to object to her extravagance, *JUDAS* bursts into the court-room. He demands an opportunity to testify on his own behalf. The court is disrupted and *JUDAS* is led away by the *BAILIFF*. Defense counsel *GRACE* asks for a recess, which is granted.

Act III
Theme: When Others Tried To Save Themselves
Prosecution counsel *JUSTICE* calls the disciple *PETER* to the witness stand. *PETER* testifies about the events surrounding Jesus' last supper, noting that Jesus waited until *JUDAS* left the room before he bestowed a special honor on the remaining disciples: that they would sit on the throne beside Jesus to judge the twelve tribes of Israel. With reference to *JUDAS*, *PETER* further testifies that a denial of Jesus is a condemnation, a denial of true life; there-fore, it leads to death. Defense counsel *GRACE* quickly gets *PE-TER* to recall that he himself denied Jesus. *PETER* tried to save himself. Was he forgiven for his denial?

Following *PETER's* testimony, *JUSTICE* calls the *YOUNG BOY* who was with Jesus during his arrest in the Garden of Gethsemane. The *YOUNG BOY* tells how *JUDAS* betrayed Jesus with a kiss; how *JUDAS* called for the authorities to take Jesus "under guard." Under gentle cross-examination by the defense, the *YOUNG BOY* admits he tried to save himself and left Jesus behind; yet he believes that Jesus forgave him. Could the same be true for *JUDAS*?

Finally, attorney *JUSTICE* calls the prosecution's last witness, *MARY*, mother of Jesus. She depicts the emotional, final moments of Jesus' death on the cross, testifying that *JUDAS* was nowhere around to ask for forgiveness. When others tried to save them-selves, Jesus did not attempt to save himself. Defense counsel *GRACE* questions *MARY* about the thieves who were crucified next to Jesus; *MARY* admits that Jesus forgave one of the thieves, and reiterates what Jesus said from the cross — "Father, forgive them, for they know not what they do" — which *GRACE* hopes to show is a blanket forgiveness to all who crucified Jesus, including *JUDAS*. Under redirect, *JUSTICE* asks *MARY* if Jesus forgave *both* thieves, to which she responds, "No." So Jesus did not forgive everyone. Prosecution rests its case, and court is recessed.

Act IV
Theme: In Bondage To Sin: We Cannot Free Ourselves
Defense begins its case by calling a *FRIEND OF JUDAS* to the witness stand. In zealous style, *FRIEND OF JUDAS* describes the traditional Jewish view of the Messiah as one who would come with power and authority and rain fire upon Israel's enemies and set up the new Kingdom of God. Defense attorney *GRACE* hopes to show that *JUDAS* could have betrayed Jesus as a way to force his hand and usher in the new Kingdom, but that *JUDAS* had made a mistake, misinterpreting Jesus' Messiahship. Prosecution counsel *JUSTICE* blasts *FRIEND OF JUDAS* under cross-examination, noting that his entire testimony is not in the scriptures; therefore, it cannot be proven. Furthermore, *JUSTICE* wonders why *JUDAS* would insist that Jesus be taken "under guard" if he thought Jesus would usher in the Kingdom.

GRACE calls the defense's next witness, *CHIEF PRIEST*. Arrogant and somewhat detached, *CHIEF PRIEST* recalls that *JUDAS* was deeply sorry for his betrayal; attorney *GRACE* implies that *JUDAS* was in bondage to sin and could not free himself — the plight of all humanity. *JUSTICE* cross-examines, and we learn that *JUDAS* wanted thirty pieces of silver to betray Jesus, suggesting that *JUDAS* was in bondage — to selfish, material gain.

For their next witness, the defense recalls *PETER* as a hostile witness. Attention is directed once again to the events of the Last Supper. At that time, did *JUDAS* partake of the Body and Blood of Christ for the forgiveness of sins? *PETER* says, "Yes." Prosecution counsel *JUSTICE* quickly shifts the focus to the Garden of Gethsemane, where *JUDAS* betrays Jesus with a kiss — a sin that occurred hours *after* the Last Supper. Court is recessed.

Act V
Theme: Who Will Save Us?

Defense counsel *GRACE* brings the *APOSTLE PAUL* to the witness stand to testify about the enormous grace of God, though we do not deserve it. Nothing can separate us from the love of God in Christ Jesus. Counselor *GRACE* hopes to show that even a person such as *JUDAS* can be forgiven by the grace of God. Prosecution attorney *JUSTICE* questions *APOSTLE PAUL*, who admits that God loves all people but that not all people are saved; we are saved by grace *through* faith.

In a dramatic climax, *GRACE* calls the final witness — *DEATH* (personified). The defense seeks to edify the meaning of the Cross and Resurrection: to forgive sins and to defeat death. The death of Christ was God's plan unto salvation — Jesus came to give us life. Defense rests. Closing arguments are given. Jury is polled. Court is adjourned.

Setting

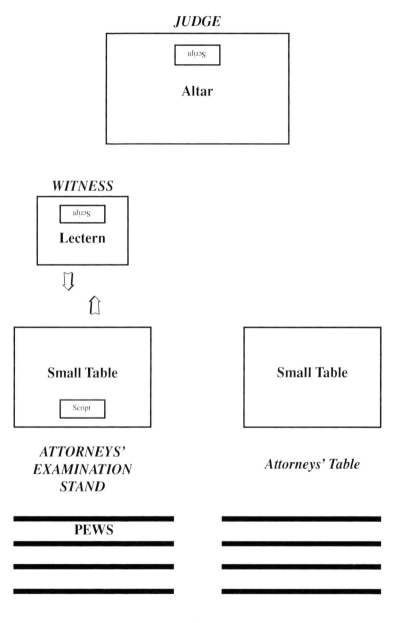

JUDGE

Script

Altar

WITNESS

Script

Lectern

Small Table

Script

Small Table

*ATTORNEYS'
EXAMINATION
STAND*

Attorneys' Table

PEWS

Lenten Service

Act I
Nothing Is Hidden From God

CONFESSION: Psalm 139:1-5, 23-24 (NRSV)
L: O Lord, you have searched me and known me.
C: You know when I sit down and when I rise up;
L: You discern my thoughts from far away.
C: You search out my path and my lying down, and are acquainted with all my ways.
L: Even before a word is on my tongue,
C: O Lord, you know it completely.
L: You hem me in, behind and before,
C: And lay your hand upon me.
L: Search me, O God, and know my heart;
C: Test me and know my thoughts.
L: See if there is any wicked way in me,
C: And lead me in the way everlasting.

CANTICLE   *The Agnus Dei*
PRAYER OF THE DAY
FIRST READING   Hebrews 4:12-16
GOSPEL READING   John 6:63-71
HYMN
DRAMA   *Opening arguments and testimony from Saint John*
OFFERING
OFFERTORY
PRAYER
LORD'S PRAYER
BENEDICTION
HYMN

Act I

Nothing Is Hidden From God

BAILIFF enters.

BAILIFF

Assertively

Please stand. You have been summoned to serve as the jury in the punishment phase of this trial. Please raise your right hand and repeat after me ...

Raise own hand and direct the congregation:

To the best of my ability ...

I pledge to be impartial ...

To listen mindfully ...

To the facts presented ...

To prayerfully consider ...

The justice and grace of God.

Lower hand

You may lower your hands. You are hereby sworn in as jurors of the Lenten District Court of _____ Church.

Loudly and quickly as JUDGE enters

Hear ye, hear ye: The Lenten District Court of _____ _____ Church is now in session, the honorable Judge I. M. Pilate presiding.

JUDGE

Casually

You may be seated.

BAILIFF takes his seat near the bench.

The following discourse is said very intensely toward the jury:

Ladies and Gentlemen, you have been duly sworn to serve as the jury. The attorneys for the Prosecution and Defense have announced ready. Attorney Justice is the prosecutor.

ATTORNEY JUSTICE stands, then sits.

And Attorney Grace is defending Mr. Judas Iscariot.

ATTORNEY GRACE stands, then sits.

This is the punishment phase of the trial of Judas Iscariot. By his own admission, he is guilty of a crime against God. Judas plead guilty to betraying innocent blood, based on the Gospel of Matthew, chapter 27, verse 4. His actions led to the death of Jesus Christ on the cross.

You are to determine the punishment of Judas. You are here to decide whether his crime against God merits eternal punishment or whether he receives God's mercy and forgiveness. God's law in this case is based on the words of Jesus in the Gospel of Mark, chapter 3, verses 28 and 29. It reads:

> *"Truly I tell you, people will be forgiven for their sins*
> *and whatever blasphemies they utter;*
> *But whoever blasphemes against the Holy Spirit*
> *can never have forgiveness,*
> *but is guilty of an eternal sin...."* (NRSV)

As the jury you are charged to determine the verdict, to set aside your own personal feelings for Judas, to listen to the facts, to weigh the credibility of the witnesses, and to prayerfully consider the justice of God's Law, which exposes our sin, and the extent of God's Grace through faith in Jesus Christ.

This court does not presume to hold our decision above God's decision. Instead, you are charged to determine whether any betrayal of God is serious enough to merit eternal punishment, in this particular case of one Judas Iscariot.

We begin the proceedings. Mr./Ms. Justice, your opening statement.

ATTORNEY JUSTICE

Takes place to address the jury (congregation)

May it please the Court, Learned Counsel, Ladies and Gentlemen of the jury. As set forth in Scripture, God's Law is meant for all of us. It's more than a set of guidelines or rules to live by. God's Law conveys truth and justice. Without it, anything goes. Without

God's Law, nothing becomes serious enough to merit any punishment at all. The prosecution will prove beyond a shadow of a doubt that Judas has committed a crime against God so serious that it merits eternal punishment.

Our evidence is the Bible itself. Our witnesses who knew the defendant will testify to several facts. Their facts are based on Scripture. You will hear evidence that Judas was evil, that he cared only for himself, that he was a thief. Reference will be made to "blood money," which we will prove is evidence of his treachery.

In summary, God desires that we turn to God with all our heart and live. If not, then punishment must be carried out or else God's justice would bear no truth at all. Thank you, your Honor.

Sits at attorneys' table

JUDGE

Mr./Ms. Grace, your opening statement.

ATTORNEY GRACE

Takes place to address the jury (congregation)

May it please the Court, Learned Counsel, Ladies and Gentlemen of the jury. Brothers and sisters, in defense of Judas Iscariot, our tradition believes that God's love and mercy is greater than our sins. The evidence to support God's mercy is — the cross! The cross is the most powerful symbol of God's love and forgiveness for a desperate, fallen humanity. I'm sure that Mr./Ms. Justice will show that Judas was a sinner. Aren't we all? The Prosecution's chief evidence is the Bible. The Bible is also our defense, the strongest evidence of forgiveness!

We will prove, based on the Bible and our witnesses, that Judas actually believed that Jesus *was* the Messiah, the Savior of the nations. His only mistake was that Judas held the traditional Jewish view of the Messiah. He really and truly did not think that Jesus *could* die. The evidence will show that Judas was attempting to get Jesus to act, to come into his power and glory, to free the people.

But Judas learned his mistake too late. Christ's power was not in a show of strength. *The power of Christ was in his dying on the cross for the sins of the world.* The testimony will bear out that even Jesus said, "Father, forgive them, for they know not what they do."

The defense will prove beyond a shadow of a doubt that nothing can separate us from the love of God — the witness of the cross — even for Judas Iscariot. Thank you, your Honor.
Sits at attorneys' table

JUDGE
Is the Prosecution prepared to begin its case?

ATTORNEY JUSTICE
Rises
Yes, your Honor. The Prosecution calls the disciple John to the witness stand.

The "oath" takes place in front of the Judge's bench; BAILIFF and JOHN cross to the front of the Judge's bench, and they face each other; ATTORNEY JUSTICE crosses to the examination stand.

BAILIFF
Raises right hand
Please raise your right hand. Do you solemnly swear to tell the truth?

JOHN
I do.
BAILIFF crosses to his seat, and JOHN crosses to the witness stand for questioning.

ATTORNEY JUSTICE
John, we apologize for disturbing you from your eternal rest to join us in this modern trial. Just a few questions. You and your brother James were disciples of Jesus. Is that correct?

JOHN
Yes. That is correct.

ATTORNEY JUSTICE
Would you tell the Court a little about yourself?

JOHN
I'm the son of Zebedee, and the younger brother of James. My family was fairly wealthy and lived in Capernaum. James and I were partners with Simon Peter in the fishing market.

ATTORNEY JUSTICE
You lived to a fairly old age, didn't you?

JOHN
Yes, the Lord blessed me with a long ministry. After years of ministry in Jerusalem, I moved to Ephesus, where I taught my disciples the teachings of Christ.

ATTORNEY JUSTICE
Is it true that when you were too weak to walk in your later years, that people would carry you to meetings, and then you would say repeatedly, "Little children, love one another"?

ATTORNEY GRACE
Objection, your Honor! Relevancy?

JUDGE
Mr./Ms. Justice, I think the Court recognizes the character of the disciple John. The jury will disregard the last question.

ATTORNEY JUSTICE
Yes, your Honor. John, as a disciple, can you tell us what Jesus was like?

JOHN
Jesus was special. You could tell it right away. Jesus is God incarnate, the word made flesh.

ATTORNEY JUSTICE

As the Son of God, could Jesus tell what you were thinking — even before you said it?

JOHN

Yes! Jesus knew every thought of our hearts. You cannot hide anything from God.

ATTORNEY JUSTICE

Did he have the same ability with Judas — to know the thoughts of his heart?

ATTORNEY GRACE

Objection. Calls for speculation.

JUDGE

Sustained. Rephrase, Mr./Ms. Justice.

ATTORNEY JUSTICE

Did Jesus say, "There are some of you who do not believe"?

JOHN

Yes. He said it about Judas.

ATTORNEY JUSTICE

What else did Jesus say about Judas?

JOHN

Jesus said, "Did I not choose twelve, and one of you is a devil?" It was obvious that Jesus knew from the very beginning that Judas was evil.

ATTORNEY JUSTICE

If Jesus knew even the thoughts of Judas' heart, is there any evidence to support that Judas was evil — other than betrayal?

JOHN

Judas was obstinate the whole three years. He was never satisfied. When he wanted to be treasurer, we agreed. But he stole from the treasury on a regular basis.

ATTORNEY JUSTICE

Did Judas do anything that might suggest any goodness in him?

JOHN

No. He was just as Jesus said. Judas was a devil.

ATTORNEY JUSTICE

Tell the Court briefly about the events of Jesus' last supper. What stood out most in your mind?

JOHN

Jesus was very distraught, very preoccupied. He talked about the suffering he was facing. We were frightened, too. In many ways it was very grim. Then Jesus did something special. He took a towel and washed our feet. He said, "I give you a new command-ment: Love one another."

ATTORNEY JUSTICE

Did Jesus say anything else connected to this foot washing?

JOHN

Jesus said that we were clean all over — all of us except one.

ATTORNEY JUSTICE

One of you was not clean?

JOHN

Judas.

ATTORNEY JUSTICE

How do you know for sure?

JOHN

Because Jesus knew that Judas would betray him.

ATTORNEY JUSTICE

No more questions, your Honor.
Takes seat

JUDGE

Mr./Ms. Grace, your witness.

ATTORNEY GRACE

Crosses to examination stand
John, would you say that Judas was the fulfillment of prophecy?

JOHN

Yes.

ATTORNEY GRACE

You testified — and I quote — that "Jesus was the embodiment of love." Does it strike you as odd that the love of God would predetermine Judas to be a betrayer?

JOHN

Arrogantly
I couldn't say.

ATTORNEY GRACE

Of course you couldn't say. You were the teacher's pet, weren't you?

ATTORNEY JUSTICE

Objection, your Honor!

JUDGE

Mr./Ms. Grace, you have been warned.

ATTORNEY GRACE

My apologies, your Honor. John, were you not the Beloved Disciple?

JOHN

Yes. Jesus said I had a special place in his heart.

ATTORNEY GRACE

Why?

JOHN

I can't say why.

ATTORNEY GRACE

Try.

JOHN

To JUDGE
Do I have to answer that?

JUDGE

Please answer the question.

JOHN

Offhandedly
I suppose because I was very young when I became a disciple. I was naive. He took me under his wing. The others would pick on me.

ATTORNEY GRACE

Did Judas ever pick on you?

JOHN

Yes.

ATTORNEY GRACE

Did that make you angry at Judas?

JOHN

It would make anyone angry.

ATTORNEY GRACE

John, were you ever known as "a son of thunder"?

JOHN

Glaring
Yes. A few people called me that to pick on me.

ATTORNEY GRACE

Is it true that you were dubbed "a son of thunder" because you had a temper problem?
JOHN refuses to answer.
Answer the question, John. Did you have a short fuse?

JOHN

Yes.

ATTORNEY GRACE

Louder
And at another time, did you argue with the other disciples that you were the greatest?

JOHN

Yes. But I was ...

ATTORNEY GRACE

Interrupting
Did you ever ask Jesus to let you sit on his right side in his glory?

JOHN

Yes.

ATTORNEY GRACE

Isn't that what you *really* wanted all along — a piece of glory?

32

JOHN

Yes. I MEAN NO!!!

ATTORNEY GRACE

Come now, John. Are you perfect?

JOHN

No. But Jesus still chose me to preach the Good News.

ATTORNEY GRACE

Did Jesus choose Judas to preach that the Kingdom of God was near?

JOHN

Yes.

ATTORNEY GRACE

Did Judas go and preach that the Kingdom of God was near?

JOHN

Yes, he did.

ATTORNEY GRACE

So in order to preach it, then Judas must have believed that the Kingdom of God was near, correct?

ATTORNEY JUSTICE

Objection. Calls for speculation. I can preach something without necessarily believing it.

ATTORNEY GRACE

To ATTORNEY JUSTICE
Which says something about your character, doesn't it?

ATTORNEY JUSTICE

Your Honor!

JUDGE
I will not have this in my court! Counselors, approach the bench.

JUSTICE and GRACE go to altar; quiet talking is overheard between the JUDGE, JUSTICE, and GRACE; then they assume their former places.

ATTORNEY GRACE
I withdraw the question. No more questions, your Honor.
Takes seat

JUDGE
Mr./Ms. Justice, care to redirect?

ATTORNEY JUSTICE
No, your Honor.

JUDGE
Very well. The witness may step down.
JOHN exits.
The Court will recess until next Wednesday night at 7:00 p.m.
JUDGE hits gavel and exits.

BAILIFF
All rise.
After JUDGE exits, say:
You may be seated. Let us continue our worship by presenting our gifts to the Lord.

Lenten Service

Act II
All Have Sinned — All Need Forgiveness

CONFESSION: Psalm 51:1, 3-4, 7-8 (NRSV)

L: Have mercy on me, O God, according to your steadfast love;

C: **According to your abundant mercy, blot out my transgressions.**

L: For I know my transgressions,

C: **And my sin is ever before me.**

L: Against you, you alone, have I sinned,

C: **And done what is evil in your sight,**

L: So that you are justified in your sentence

C: **And blameless when you pass judgment.**

L: Purge me with hyssop, and I shall be clean;

C: **Wash me, and I shall be whiter than snow.**

L: Let me hear joy and gladness;

C: **Let the bones that you have crushed rejoice.**

CANTICLE	*The Agnus Dei*
PRAYER OF THE DAY	
FIRST READING	Romans 2:1-4
GOSPEL READING	Matthew 26:3-16
HYMN	
DRAMA	*Testimony of Mary Magdalene and the Unnamed Woman*
OFFERING	
OFFERTORY	
PRAYER	
LORD'S PRAYER	
BENEDICTION	
HYMN	

Act II

All Have Sinned — All Need Forgiveness

BAILIFF enters.

BAILIFF

All rise.
Loudly and quickly as JUDGE enters
Hear ye, hear ye: The Lenten District Court of _____
_____ Church is now in session, the honorable Judge I. M.
Pilate presiding.

JUDGE

JUDGE sits.
You may be seated.
BAILIFF takes his seat near the bench.
Mr./Ms. Justice, is the Prosecution ready to continue with the pro-
ceedings?

ATTORNEY JUSTICE

Yes, your Honor. If it pleases the Court, the Prosection calls Mary
Magdalene to the witness stand.

*The "oath" takes place in front of the Judge's bench; BAILIFF
and MARY MAGDALENE cross to the front of the Judge's bench,
and they face each other; ATTORNEY JUSTICE crosses to the
examination stand.*

BAILIFF

Raises right hand
Please raise your right hand. Do you solemnly swear to tell the
truth?

MARY MAGDALENE

I do.

BAILIFF crosses to his seat, and MARY MAGDALENE crosses to the witness stand for questioning.

ATTORNEY JUSTICE
Mary, welcome to our century. We appreciate your willingness to leave your heavenly home to appear in this court.

MARY MAGDALENE
No problem, Counselor.

ATTORNEY JUSTICE
For the record, is Magdalene your last name?

MARY MAGDALENE
No. I'm called Magdalene because I was from the town of Magdala.

ATTORNEY JUSTICE
Were you a follower of Jesus Christ and his ministry?

MARY MAGDALENE
I sure was.

ATTORNEY JUSTICE
And did you know the defendant, Judas Iscariot?

MARY MAGDALENE
Unfortunately, yes, I did. I knew the man all too well.

ATTORNEY JUSTICE
How did you come to be a follower of Jesus?

MARY MAGDALENE
Well, I was in a really bad way. If ever anybody was lost — it was me! I needed God to give me a new life.

Then I heard about Jesus. Everyone was talking about him! When he came to our village preaching the Good News, I met him.

I was healed instantly. I had a new life. I mean, it's not like I was an angel after that, but I was different.

ATTORNEY JUSTICE
Did you go about your way after Jesus came into your life?

MARY MAGDALENE
No way! I couldn't. Jesus asked me to help spread the Good News. He did the same with many of the men and women he healed. Whenever Jesus healed, people followed.

ATTORNEY JUSTICE
How long did you stay with the disciples and Jesus?

MARY MAGDALENE
All the way to the cross and the empty tomb, Counselor. When the disciples ran scared, I stayed at the foot of the cross.

ATTORNEY JUSTICE
Did Judas also run away?

MARY MAGDALENE
You've got to be joking! Judas betrayed our Lord in the first place. He had every reason to run. He put Jesus on the cross.

ATTORNEY GRACE
Objection. Assumes facts not in evidence! The witness' last remark assumes that Jesus would not have been crucified if it weren't for Judas. Please instruct the jury to disregard the last statement.

ATTORNEY JUSTICE
Your Honor, the witness was simply stating a consequence of Judas' betrayal. It led to the death of Jesus.

ATTORNEY GRACE
Judas betrayed Jesus. He did not physically put Jesus on the cross! The authorities did that.

JUDGE
I will sustain the objection. The jury will disregard the last statement by the witness.

ATTORNEY JUSTICE
What was Judas like during those ministry years?

MARY MAGDALENE
Shakes her head
Man, you wouldn't believe it. Iscariot was a real pain. He constantly complained — which *didn't* seem to surprise Jesus too much. I think Jesus just expected it.

ATTORNEY JUSTICE
When he betrayed Jesus, did you ever hear him ask for forgiveness?

MARY MAGDALENE
Absolutely not.

ATTORNEY JUSTICE
Did you ever hear Jesus forgive Judas?

MARY MAGDALENE
No.

ATTORNEY JUSTICE
Did Jesus say anything else about Judas?

MARY MAGDALENE
He said one of the disciples was *a devil*. And the Betrayer had no faith. That's what Jesus said.

ATTORNEY JUSTICE
Thank you, Mary. No more questions, your Honor.
Takes seat

JUDGE
Mr./Ms. Grace, your witness.

ATTORNEY GRACE
Crosses to examination stand
Mary Magdalene, you gave quite a testimony! May I remind you
that you are under oath? Can *everything* you said be proven in the
Bible?

MARY MAGDALENE
First of all, you don't have to remind me anything. Second, everything I said was true!

ATTORNEY GRACE
For instance, you testified that Judas complained constantly. Where
is that in the Bible?

MARY MAGDALENE
It's in there all right. Like when he complained about the Unnamed Woman anointing Jesus' feet.

ATTORNEY GRACE
You're right. But that's the *only* place, isn't it? Did the other
disciples ever complain?

MARY MAGDALENE
Sighs
Yes.

ATTORNEY GRACE
You testified that you were present during the crucifixion. Did
Jesus complain?

MARY MAGDALENE
No. In fact, he asked the Father to forgive them.

ATTORNEY GRACE
So Jesus wanted to forgive the people who crucified him?

MARY MAGDALENE
Yes, but remember that Jesus once said Iscariot was a devil. Is the devil ever forgiven?

ATTORNEY GRACE
Well, let's talk about forgiveness. You testified that Jesus healed you. Healed you from what?

MARY MAGDALENE
He cast out seven demons from me.

ATTORNEY GRACE
So what were your demons?

MARY MAGDALENE
I refuse to answer that question on the grounds that it might incriminate me.

ATTORNEY GRACE
Come now, Mary. Hear the words of Jesus, "Judge not, that you be not judged...." Didn't you also need forgiveness?

MARY MAGDALENE
We *all* need forgiveness — including you!

ATTORNEY GRACE
So you're saying that we are all sinners, correct?

MARY MAGDALENE
That's right.

ATTORNEY GRACE
Including Judas?

MARY MAGDALENE
Yes.

ATTORNEY GRACE
And you're saying we all need forgiveness, right?

MARY MAGDALENE
Yes.

ATTORNEY GRACE
Including Judas?

MARY MAGDALENE
Yes.

ATTORNEY GRACE
And what did Jesus say from the cross about forgiveness?

MARY MAGDALENE
"Father, forgive them, for they know not what they do."

ATTORNEY GRACE
Thank you, Mary. No more questions, your Honor.
Takes seat

JUDGE
Care to redirect, Mr./Ms. Justice?

ATTORNEY JUSTICE
No questions, your Honor.

JUDGE
The witness may step down. The Prosecution may call its next witness.
MARY MAGDALENE exits.

ATTORNEY JUSTICE
Crosses to examination stand
Your Honor, if it pleases the Court, the Prosecution calls the Un-named Woman to the witness stand.

The "oath" takes place in front of the Judge's bench; BAILIFF and UNNAMED WOMAN cross to the front of the Judge's bench, and they face each other; ATTORNEY JUSTICE crosses to the examination stand.

BAILIFF

Raises right hand
Please raise your right hand. Do you solemnly swear to tell the truth?

UNNAMED WOMAN
I do.
BAILIFF crosses to his seat, and UNNAMED WOMAN crosses to the witness stand for questioning.

ATTORNEY JUSTICE
You are known as "The Unnamed Woman" from the Gospels of Matthew and Mark, are you not?

UNNAMED WOMAN
Yes, I am.

ATTORNEY JUSTICE
For the record, will you please state your given name?

UNNAMED WOMAN
I am Mary of Bethany, sister of Martha, and sister of Lazarus, whom Jesus raised from the dead.

ATTORNEY JUSTICE
For the Court, why are you known as "The Unnamed Woman" if you are Mary of Bethany?

UNNAMED WOMAN

The Gospels of Matthew and Mark did not call me by name. There-fore, I was the "Unnamed Woman."

ATTORNEY JUSTICE

How is it that you came to know Jesus?

UNNAMED WOMAN

My family and Jesus were good friends, so he visited often.

ATTORNEY JUSTICE

You are known for a very special act, aren't you? In fact, Jesus said, "Truly I say to you, wherever the gospel is preached in the whole world, what she has done will be told in memory of her."

ATTORNEY GRACE

Objection, your Honor. Bolstering the witness.

JUDGE

Sustained. Rephrase, Mr./Ms. Justice.

ATTORNEY JUSTICE

Mary, what did you do that was so "unique"?

UNNAMED WOMAN

I anointed Jesus with oil.

ATTORNEY JUSTICE

Why?

UNNAMED WOMAN

Since Jesus was the King of the Universe, he deserved to be anointed. But I also knew from listening to him that he was about to die. By anointing Jesus, I also prepared his body for burial, because perfumed oils were used to anoint bodies after death.

ATTORNEY JUSTICE
Now, tell us what transpired.

UNNAMED WOMAN
A few days before the Passover, Jesus and his disciples stopped by to visit. My brother Lazarus and Jesus were very close, and I think Jesus was really coming by to say goodbye. Jesus was very anxious and I could tell he was frightened.

While my sister Martha served supper, I took a pound of ointment, made of pure nard, and anointed Jesus' feet. Then I wiped it off with my hair.

ATTORNEY JUSTICE
What exactly is "nard"?

UNNAMED WOMAN
It's an ointment prepared from the roots and stems of an herb from India. It's for very rare occasions.

ATTORNEY JUSTICE
Was Judas there to see this?

UNNAMED WOMAN
Yes, he was.

ATTORNEY JUSTICE
Did you notice a reaction from him?

UNNAMED WOMAN
Definitely. He became very angry at me. He accused me of wasting the oil.

ATTORNEY JUSTICE
Wasting the oil?

UNNAMED WOMAN

Yes, *wasting* the oil on Jesus. He said I could have sold it for 300 denarii and given the money to the poor.

ATTORNEY JUSTICE

How did you respond?

UNNAMED WOMAN

I was pretty emotional that evening. I was sad about losing Jesus. So when Judas scolded me, I started to cry.

ATTORNEY JUSTICE

Did Jesus respond to Judas?

UNNAMED WOMAN

Yes. Jesus defended me!

ATTORNEY JUSTICE

How so?

UNNAMED WOMAN

Very emphatically, as I recall. He told Judas to leave me alone. I think Jesus was touched by what I had done for him, and it made him angry that Judas was scolding me.

ATTORNEY JUSTICE

How did Judas react after Jesus admonished him? Did he apologize?

UNNAMED WOMAN

No. He stormed out of the room.

ATTORNEY JUSTICE

Does the Bible say anything about where Judas went after he left your house?

UNNAMED WOMAN

Yes. He went to the chief priests.

ATTORNEY JUSTICE

Why?

UNNAMED WOMAN

He wanted to hand Jesus over to them.

ATTORNEY JUSTICE

Thank you, Mary. No more questions, your Honor.

JUDGE

Mr./Ms. Grace, your witness.

ATTORNEY GRACE

Crosses to examination stand

Mary, you testified that the ointment was worth 300 denarii. In today's American money, that comes to about $22,000 poured out in a single moment. Doesn't that seem expensive?

UNNAMED WOMAN

As I said before, Jesus was not just a man. He was the King of the Universe who — I might add — was about to die.

ATTORNEY GRACE

Mary, I couldn't agree with you more. But was Judas the *only* person that night who objected when you poured out $22,000 worth of ointment?

UNNAMED WOMAN

No.

ATTORNEY GRACE

According to Matthew and Mark, *several* disciples objected, didn't they?

UNNAMED WOMAN
Yes.

ATTORNEY GRACE
Thank you, Mary. No more questions, your Honor.
Takes seat.

JUDAS
JUDAS bursts into courtroom.
You're all sinners! You're all sinners!

JUDGE
JUDGE hits gavel.
Order! Order in the court!

Simultaneously:

JUDAS	JUDGE
All of you are alike! You need forgiveness, too! You're no better than me!	Bailiff! Remove the Defendant. Order in the court!

JUDAS	
No! I want to testify! I *need* to testify. Give me a chance! Sinners! You need forgiveness!	*BAILIFF begins to remove JUDAS.*
	BAILIFF and JUDAS exit.

ATTORNEY JUSTICE
To ATTORNEY GRACE
Do something to control your client! Obviously, Judas Iscariot has no regard for rules in a courtroom.

ATTORNEY GRACE
Your Honor, please advise that I do not take instructions from the Counselor. I take instructions from the bench.

JUDGE
Well, control your client!

ATTORNEY GRACE

Your Honor, the defense requests a recess so I may consult with my client, Mr. Iscariot.

JUDGE

Very well. The court will recess until next Wednesday night at 7:00 p.m.
JUDGE hits gavel and exits.

BAILIFF

All rise.
After JUDGE exits, say:
You may be seated. Let us continue our worship and present our gifts to the Lord.

Lenten Service

Act III
When Others Tried To Save Themselves

CONFESSION: Psalm 25:16-18, 20-21 (NRSV)

L: Turn to me and be gracious to me,

C: For I am lonely and afflicted.

L: Relieve the troubles of my heart,

C: And bring me out of my distress.

L: Consider my affliction and my trouble,

C: And forgive all my sins.

L: O guard my life and deliver me;

C: Do not let me be put to shame, for I take refuge in you.

L: May integrity and uprightness preserve me,

C: For I wait for you.

CANTICLE	*The Agnus Dei*
PRAYER OF THE DAY	
FIRST READING	Galatians 5:16-25
GOSPEL READING	Mark 14:53-54, 66-72
HYMN	
DRAMA	*Prosecution rests after testimony from Saint Peter, the Young Boy, and Mary*
OFFERING	
OFFERTORY	
PRAYER	
LORD'S PRAYER	
BENEDICTION	
HYMN	

Act III

When Others Tried To Save Themselves

BAILIFF enters.

BAILIFF

All rise.
Loudly and quickly as JUDGE enters
Hear ye, hear ye: The Lenten District Court of _____ _____ Church is now in session, the Honorable Judge I. M. Pilate presiding.

JUDGE

JUDGE sits.
You may be seated.
BAILIFF takes his seat near the bench.
Mr./Ms. Grace, I assume you straightened out that little incident with Mr. Iscariot?

ATTORNEY GRACE

Yes, your Honor.

JUDGE

Thank you. As to you, Mr./Ms. Justice, as you so clearly pointed out, there are rules in court, and one of those rules is that I — not you — am in charge here. I — not you — will deliver instructions in this court. Are those rules clear?

ATTORNEY JUSTICE

My apologies, your Honor. I beg the Court's forgiveness.

JUDGE

We'll have to see about that. At any rate, no more disruptions in my court from *either side*. Now, Mr./Ms. Justice, is the Prosecution ready to continue with the proceedings?

ATTORNEY JUSTICE

Yes, your Honor. If it pleases the Court, the Prosecution calls the disciple Peter to the witness stand.

The "oath" takes place in front of the Judge's bench; BAILIFF and PETER cross to the front of the Judge's bench, and they face each other; ATTORNEY JUSTICE crosses to the examination stand.

BAILIFF

Raises right hand
Please raise your right hand. Do you solemnly swear to tell the truth?

PETER

I do.
PETER takes seat at the witness stand; BAILIFF returns to his seat.

ATTORNEY JUSTICE

Peter, welcome to our century. Did you know the defendant, Judas Iscariot?

PETER

Yes, I did!

ATTORNEY JUSTICE

How would you describe him?

PETER

The best way to describe Judas was by what he did. He betrayed the Son of God, and caused him a lot of suffering on the cross.

ATTORNEY JUSTICE

Did Jesus ever say anything about the character of Judas?

PETER

Jesus said a lot of things about Judas. He said that Judas did not believe, that he was not all clean, and that he was a devil. Jesus also said that Judas would fulfill the Scriptures. On top of all this, I would add that he was a thief.

ATTORNEY JUSTICE

Did Jesus mention anything about forgiving Judas?

PETER

Not that I heard. In fact, he said just the opposite.

ATTORNEY JUSTICE

What did Jesus say?

PETER

He said, "Woe to the one who betrays the Son of Man! It would have been better for that one not to have been born."

ATTORNEY JUSTICE

Are you absolutely certain that he was talking about Judas?

PETER

Without a doubt! Because Judas — being the coward that he was — tried to hide his actions. He turned to Jesus and asked, "Surely, not I, Rabbi!" And Jesus said, "You have said so."

ATTORNEY JUSTICE

When did this conversation take place, Peter?

PETER

At the Passover meal, the night before Jesus was nailed to the cross.

ATTORNEY JUSTICE

For the Court, please describe the events of that last supper.

PETER

It was a very still night, no breeze, and the paschal moon was very bright that night. We were all frightened of every shadow, every bump in the room. Jesus was probably the most upset. He knew he was going to die — and very painfully. We were all trying to reassure him, but it wasn't doing any good because we were just as scared.

While we were eating, Jesus took a loaf of bread and told us all to share it, that it was his body. Then he took the cup of wine and told us that it was his blood, shed for us.

ATTORNEY JUSTICE

Then what happened?

PETER

At the time I wasn't sure what was happening, but Jesus told Judas to leave and get it over with, and Judas left. With that fox out of the room, Jesus said a few more things about how we would some-day sit on the throne beside him to judge the twelve tribes of Israel.

ATTORNEY JUSTICE

So Jesus waited until Judas was out of the room to disclose this high honor?

PETER

Yes.

ATTORNEY JUSTICE

What happened next?

PETER

We went to the Mount of Olives for a while, then on to the Garden of Gethsemane.

ATTORNEY JUSTICE

So Judas waited to hand over Jesus until you were at the Garden of Gethsemane?

PETER

With anger!
Yes! He knew there would be no one around to put up a fight!

ATTORNEY GRACE

Objection, your Honor. The answer is sheer speculation. Request that the jury be instructed.

ATTORNEY JUSTICE

Your Honor, we're trying to establish the nature of the betrayal. These are documented facts.

ATTORNEY GRACE

Your Honor, who can document what goes on in someone else's mind? It's ridiculous.

PETER

Ridiculous?!! Who's he calling ridiculous?

JUDGE

Hits gavel
I will have order here! Mr./Ms. Grace, your objection is overruled.

ATTORNEY GRACE

Please note my exception!

JUDGE

Exception noted. Proceed, Mr./Ms. Justice.

ATTORNEY JUSTICE

Thank you, your Honor. Peter, did Jesus ever talk about an unforgivable sin?

PETER

Yes. He said that anyone who denies the Holy Spirit never has forgiveness, because he has committed an eternal sin.

ATTORNEY JUSTICE

Then, since Jesus and the Holy Spirit are one God with the Father, would you say that denying Jesus is an eternal sin?

PETER

Judas denied the Holy and Righteous One, and his betrayal caused the Author of Life to die a horrible death on the cross. To deny Jesus is to deny true life. So to answer your question, I think that a denial of Jesus *is* a condemnation.

ATTORNEY JUSTICE

Thank you, Peter. No more questions, your Honor.
Sits at table

JUDGE

Mr./Ms. Grace, your witness.

ATTORNEY GRACE

Crosses to examination stand
Peter, are you in heaven?

ATTORNEY JUSTICE

Objection, your Honor!

ATTORNEY GRACE

Your Honor, what's the counselor's problem?

JUDGE

The question is, "Where are you going with this line of questioning?"

ATTORNEY GRACE

Your Honor, I'm entitled to know and it would be most beneficial for the Court to know the basis of Mr./Ms. Justice's objection. However, out of respect, I will show the Court that I have a very relevant road to travel here.

ATTORNEY JUSTICE
Yes, let's just hope it's not a dead-end road!

JUDGE
Watch yourself, Mr./Ms. Justice. I'll overrule the objection. But Mr./Ms. Grace, keep the road short.

ATTORNEY GRACE
Thank you, your Honor. Peter, are you in heaven?

PETER
I am with Jesus.

ATTORNEY GRACE
That's interesting. According to your testimony, you should be in a very, very warm place. You implied that anyone who denies Jesus has no forgiveness. And yet, you denied Jesus — how many times was it? Three times, I believe, did you not?

PETER
Well ... It wasn't the same thing.

ATTORNEY GRACE
Oh, no? When you did it, you even cursed, did you not?
Pause
When you were at the High Priest's house warming yourself nice and cozy by the fire while Jesus was about to die, and you yourself were being accused, did you not say, "I tell you I don't know that 'blankety blank' man"?

PETER
I tell you it wasn't the same as Judas!

ATTORNEY GRACE
Careful, Peter. The cock is about to crow again! Do you remember the sound of that rooster crowing? Do you remember how *you* denied Jesus?

PETER

Covers his face
Yes. Yes. I felt so ashamed!

ATTORNEY GRACE

It's okay, Peter. We all deny Jesus in one way or another, don't we? But did you not write these words? "Christ bore our sins in his body on the cross.... By his wounds you have been healed"!

PETER

Looking up
But Judas crucified him for thirty pieces of silver!

ATTORNEY GRACE

How do you think Jesus felt when you denied him? Don't you think every word from your mouth that night in the courtyard put a nail right through his heart? Isn't it true that *we all* crucified Jesus?

PETER

Jesus warned me that night. He said that Satan wanted me, but that he would pray for me.

ATTORNEY GRACE

Peter, doesn't Satan want all of us?
Pause
No more questions, your Honor.
Takes seat

JUDGE

Care to redirect, Mr./Ms. Justice?

ATTORNEY JUSTICE

Yes, your Honor.
Crosses to examination stand
You sinned that night in the courtyard. Did you ask God for forgiveness?

PETER

Head down, reflective
With all my heart.

ATTORNEY JUSTICE

So what would you say was the difference between your denial and that of Judas?

PETER

I asked for forgiveness and waited. I kept strong in the faith.

ATTORNEY JUSTICE

No more questions, your Honor.

JUDGE

The witness may step down. Mr./Ms. Justice? The Prosecution's next witness?
PETER exits

ATTORNEY JUSTICE

Crosses to examination stand
Your Honor, if it pleases the Court, the Prosecution calls the Young Boy to the witness stand.

The "oath" takes place in front of the Judge's bench; BAILIFF and YOUNG BOY cross to the front of the Judge's bench, and they face each other; ATTORNEY JUSTICE crosses to the examination stand.

BAILIFF

Please raise your right hand...
BAILIFF raises hand also.
Do you solemnly swear to tell the truth?

YOUNG BOY

I do.

BAILIFF crosses to his seat, and YOUNG BOY crosses to the witness stand for questioning.

ATTORNEY JUSTICE
In the Gospel of Mark, you are known simply as "The Young Boy," are you not?

YOUNG BOY
Yes, sir/ma'am.

ATTORNEY JUSTICE
Why does Mark talk about you in his Gospel?

YOUNG BOY
I was there when they arrested Jesus. I saw the whole thing.

ATTORNEY JUSTICE
Why were you there that night?

YOUNG BOY
Sometimes I would go to the Garden to listen to Jesus. I knew he would be there.

ATTORNEY JUSTICE
Would you tell us what you saw that night?

YOUNG BOY
Jesus was praying pretty hard, and he asked the disciples to stay awake with him. But they kept falling asleep.

Then we saw these lights coming — a whole bunch of them, like stars moving over the land. I wasn't sure what was going on, but Jesus knew. He said it was time. I started to get really scared.

ATTORNEY JUSTICE
Did you get a good look at the crowd?

YOUNG BOY

Yes, sir/ma'am. It was a big crowd. There were Roman soldiers and officers of the Jewish Temple Police.

ATTORNEY JUSTICE

Were they armed?

YOUNG BOY

Yes, sir/ma'am. They had clubs and swords. It was really scary!

ATTORNEY JUSTICE

Then what happened?

YOUNG BOY

Well, I'm pretty sure that Judas was out in front of the crowd, because he ran up to Jesus and said, "Hello, Teacher!" Then Judas kissed him on the cheek. That's when some of them jumped on Jesus.

ATTORNEY JUSTICE

Then what happened?

YOUNG BOY

Then I heard Judas yell, "Better take him under guard!" So they tied up his hands.

ATTORNEY JUSTICE

Did any of the disciples fight for Jesus?

YOUNG BOY

Yes, sir/ma'am. Peter did. He drew out his sword and swung it *(demonstrates)* and he cut off somebody's ear. I think it was the High Priest's slave, Malchus.

ATTORNEY JUSTICE

What happened next?

YOUNG BOY

Well, sir/ma'am, I couldn't say for sure, but I think Judas yelled at the guards to capture the disciples. All I know for sure was that the guards started coming after the disciples and me.

ATTORNEY JUSTICE

After you, too?

YOUNG BOY

Yes, sir/ma'am. They went after us like madmen. We scattered like a bunch of ants. I almost didn't get away myself.

ATTORNEY JUSTICE

Why?

YOUNG BOY

A guard grabbed my linen cloth, and I wrestled as hard as I could. I didn't want to die. The cloth came off of me and I ran away naked.

ATTORNEY JUSTICE

You're saying that all this started when Judas kissed Jesus?

YOUNG BOY

Yes, sir/ma'am. The kiss of betrayal.

ATTORNEY JUSTICE

Thank you, young man. No more questions, your Honor.

JUDGE

Mr./Ms. Grace, your witness.

ATTORNEY GRACE

Crosses to examination stand
You're doing a really fine job, young man. Are you nervous?

YOUNG BOY

Yes, sir/ma'am. A little.

ATTORNEY GRACE

Were you this nervous that night at the Garden?

YOUNG BOY

Even more that night!

ATTORNEY GRACE

Being that scared, did you pay much attention to the expression on Judas' face?

YOUNG BOY

No, not really.

ATTORNEY GRACE

So Judas could have looked sorry and you just didn't see it, right?

YOUNG BOY

I guess so.

ATTORNEY GRACE

After you ran away from Jesus, do you think Jesus forgave you?

YOUNG BOY

I think so. Jesus was very nice. Whenever we did something wrong, he forgave us.

ATTORNEY GRACE

Judas did something very wrong that night, didn't he?

YOUNG BOY

Yes, sir/ma'am.

ATTORNEY GRACE

And Jesus forgave you that night, right?

YOUNG BOY

Yes, sir/ma'am. I believe it in my heart.

ATTORNEY GRACE

No more questions, your Honor.
Takes seat.

JUDGE

Thank you, young man. You may step down.
YOUNG BOY exits.

ATTORNEY JUSTICE

Your Honor, if it pleases the Court, the Prosecution calls Mary, the
Mother of Jesus, to the witness stand.

*The "oath" takes place in front of the Judge's bench; BAILIFF
and MARY cross to the front of the Judge's bench, and they face
each other; ATTORNEY JUSTICE crosses to the examination stand.*

BAILIFF

Please raise your right hand.
BAILIFF raises hand also.
Do you solemnly swear to tell the truth?

MARY

I do.
*BAILIFF crosses to his seat, and MARY crosses to the witness stand
for questioning.*

ATTORNEY JUSTICE

Mary, as the Scriptures proclaim, you are to be called "Blessed"
because you are the mother of Jesus, our Lord. This blessing is
quite an honor. You must have been very happy.

MARY

I was honored, but I have discovered that being blessed doesn't
always mean happiness.

ATTORNEY JUSTICE
Can you tell us more about that?

MARY
I wasn't very happy to see my son hanging on a cross. When they drove nails in his body, they may as well have driven them in my heart.

ATTORNEY JUSTICE
I know this will be difficult for you, but for the Court, please describe the events of Jesus' death.

MARY
After Judas betrayed him, they tried him before a mock court of the Sanhedrin. Then they handed him over to Pilate. Then they dragged him before the festival, and I thought he would be released, but the crowd kept shouting ...
Pauses, looks down, and puts hand over her face as if to choke back tears
But the crowd shouted, "Crucify him! Crucify him!"

ATTORNEY JUSTICE
During all this, did you ever see Judas around?

MARY
No. He was nowhere.

ATTORNEY JUSTICE
After the crowd yelled, "Crucify him!" what happened then?

MARY
They took Jesus ... they stripped off his clothes and put on an old purple cloak from Pilate's court. Then they put on a crown made of briar thorns. He was bleeding down his face.

After they made fun of Jesus, they beat him and made him carry his cross.

When they got to the hill along the road, they drove nails into his hands and feet. I've never heard him scream like that before. It took three men to hold him down.

ATTORNEY JUSTICE
Then what happened?

MARY
I didn't pay attention to details. I watched my son die — painfully and slowly and without a shred of dignity!

When they let him down, I cradled his lifeless body until they had to pull me away.

ATTORNEY JUSTICE
And you said that Judas Iscariot was not around?

MARY
With deep feeling, eyes closed
No! He was nowhere to be found.

ATTORNEY JUSTICE
Thank you, Mary. No more questions, your Honor.
Takes seat

JUDGE
Mr./Ms. Grace, your witness.

ATTORNEY GRACE
Crosses to examination stand
Mary, please forgive me, but while Jesus was on the cross, and enduring so much pain, did he attempt to save himself?

MARY
No. He never did.

ATTORNEY GRACE

But we heard testimony tonight that others tried to save their own skin. The disciples scattered. The Young Boy ran away. And even Peter denied that he knew Jesus. These folks all tried to save themselves. Why didn't Jesus save himself?

MARY

He lived and died to save others — not himself.

ATTORNEY GRACE

Mary, was Jesus the only one who was crucified that day?

MARY

No. There were two others.

ATTORNEY GRACE

Did Jesus talk to them while he was dying?

MARY

He talked to the one on his right.

ATTORNEY GRACE

What did they talk about?

MARY

The man said he was sorry for the things he had done and that he was getting what he deserved, but that Jesus did not deserve to die, because he had done nothing wrong.

ATTORNEY GRACE

Did Jesus say anything to the man?

MARY

Jesus said, "Today you will be with me in paradise."

ATTORNEY GRACE
So Jesus forgave this man — this terrible sinner who deserved to die?

MARY
Yes.

ATTORNEY GRACE
Did Jesus say anything else that night about forgiveness?

MARY
Yes. When they first put him on the cross, Jesus said, "Father, forgive them, for they know not what they do."

ATTORNEY GRACE
Thank you, Mary. No more questions, your Honor.
Takes seat

ATTORNEY JUSTICE
Redirect, your Honor.
Crosses to examination stand
Mary, did Jesus forgive the other man on his left?

MARY
No.

ATTORNEY JUSTICE
So Jesus did not forgive everyone there that night, did he?

MARY
No. He didn't.

ATTORNEY JUSTICE
No more questions. The Prosecution rests, your Honor.

JUDGE

Mary, you may step down.

MARY exits.

The court will recess until next Wednesday night at 7:00. At that time, the Defense can begin its case.

JUDGE hits gavel and exits.

BAILIFF

All rise.

After JUDGE exits, say:

You may be seated. Let us continue our worship by presenting our gifts to the Lord.

Lenten Service

Act IV
In Bondage To Sin: We Cannot Free Ourselves

CONFESSION: Psalm 25:1-2a, 4-7, 11 (NRSV)

L: To you, O Lord, I lift up my soul.

C: **O my God, in you I trust.**

L: Make me know your ways, O Lord;

C: **Teach me your paths.**

L: Lead me in your truth, and teach me,

C: **For you are the God of my salvation; for you I wait all day long.**

L: Be mindful of your mercy, O Lord, and of your steadfast love,

C: **For they have been from of old.**

L: Do not remember the sins of my youth or my transgressions;

C: **According to your steadfast love remember me.**

L: For your name's sake, O Lord,

C: **Pardon my guilt, for it is great.**

CANTICLE   *The Agnus Dei*
PRAYER OF THE DAY
FIRST READING   Hebrews 12:14-17
GOSPEL READING   Matthew 27:1-10
HYMN
DRAMA   *The Defense's case begins with testimony from Friend of Judas, Chief Priest, and Saint Peter (recalled)*

OFFERING
OFFERTORY
PRAYER
LORD'S PRAYER
BENEDICTION
HYMN

73

Act IV

In Bondage To Sin: We Cannot Free Ourselves

BAILIFF enters.

BAILIFF

All rise.
Loudly and quickly as JUDGE enters
Hear ye, hear ye: The Lenten District Court of _____
_____ Church is now in session, the Honorable Judge I. M.
Pilate presiding.

JUDGE

JUDGE sits.
You may be seated.
BAILIFF takes his seat near the bench.
The Prosecution has ended its case. Mr./Ms. Grace, is the Defense
prepared to present its case?

ATTORNEY GRACE

Yes, your Honor. If it pleases the Court, the Defense calls its first
witness: a Friend of Judas Iscariot.

*The "oath" takes place in front of the Judge's bench; BAILIFF
and FRIEND OF JUDAS cross to the front of the Judge's bench,
and they face each other; ATTORNEY GRACE crosses to the examination stand.*

BAILIFF

Raises right hand
Please raise your right hand. Do you solemnly swear to tell the
truth?

FRIEND OF JUDAS

I do.

FRIEND OF JUDAS takes seat at the witness stand; BAILIFF returns to his seat.

ATTORNEY GRACE
Friend of Judas, welcome to our century. Did you know the defendant, Judas Iscariot?

FRIEND OF JUDAS
Yes.

ATTORNEY GRACE
How long did you know Judas?

FRIEND OF JUDAS
Since we were teenagers. We were close friends.

ATTORNEY GRACE
What was the nature of your friendship?

FRIEND OF JUDAS
We shared the same religious and political views. We were both zealots.

ATTORNEY GRACE
What do you mean by "zealots"?

FRIEND OF JUDAS
We were both interested in the freedom of Israel. God Almighty gave us the Promised Land, and those pagan Romans were in our land. We zealots were dedicated to getting them out and setting free the people of God!
Waves hand with a fist.

ATTORNEY GRACE
So Judas was a zealot, dedicated to the freedom of Israel. Did zealots like yourself and Judas believe that the Messiah would come?

FRIEND OF JUDAS
Of course!

ATTORNEY GRACE
What did you believe the Messiah would do?

FRIEND OF JUDAS
The Messiah was to come in a show of strength, to rain fire from heaven, and to set up the new Kingdom of God.

ATTORNEY GRACE
So the Messiah was supposed to be all-powerful, correct?

FRIEND OF JUDAS
Yes — to free God's people from the oppressive, Roman occupation of the Holy Land.

ATTORNEY GRACE
Did you ever have any conversations with Judas during the years that he was a disciple of Jesus?

FRIEND OF JUDAS
Many.

ATTORNEY GRACE
In those conversations, did Judas ever mention that he believed Jesus was the Messiah?

FRIEND OF JUDAS
He said many times that Jesus had the power to set Israel free.

ATTORNEY GRACE
Now, we all know that Judas betrayed Jesus. But did Judas ever give you any indication that he was impatient with Jesus?

FRIEND OF JUDAS

On many occasions Judas said that Jesus was not bold enough. He said that Jesus needed to act — and act now — to free the people of Israel.

ATTORNEY GRACE

Is it true that he betrayed Jesus in order to force him into his Messiahship?

FRIEND OF JUDAS

Yes. He said that he would have to force Jesus to act, to bring in the Kingdom of God, to free the Chosen People of God! He betrayed him to force him to act.

ATTORNEY GRACE

But the traditional Jewish view of the Messiah was wrong — and Jesus died on the cross instead, correct?

FRIEND OF JUDAS

But Judas could not have known that Jesus would die. We didn't think the Messiah could die.

ATTORNEY GRACE

Thank you, Friend of Judas. No more questions, your Honor.
Takes seat

JUDGE

Mr./Ms. Justice, your witness.

ATTORNEY JUSTICE

Crosses to examination stand
Friend of Judas, did you believe that Judas had good intentions?

FRIEND OF JUDAS

Yes, I did!

ATTORNEY JUSTICE

Did you believe that good intentions could excuse his behavior?

FRIEND OF JUDAS

Yes.

ATTORNEY JUSTICE

So it doesn't matter how harmful we are to other people, so long as we have good intentions? Is that what you're saying?

FRIEND OF JUDAS

I'm not sure.

ATTORNEY JUSTICE

Friend of Judas, where are you written about in Scripture?

FRIEND OF JUDAS

I am not in the Bible.

ATTORNEY JUSTICE

So we cannot prove anything you said about Judas. Where in the Bible does it say that Judas believed Jesus was the Messiah?

FRIEND OF JUDAS

I don't think it says that — but he told me.

ATTORNEY JUSTICE

The Bible does have a few things to say about Judas — that he was a devil, that he was a thief, that he only cared for himself. Did he ever tell you these things about himself?

FRIEND OF JUDAS

No.

ATTORNEY JUSTICE

So Judas comes up to you and says that Jesus is the long-awaited Messiah, but does he tell you that Judas himself was an evil, self-centered cheat?

FRIEND OF JUDAS

Why would he? He didn't think he *was*.

ATTORNEY JUSTICE

So we have the authoritative word of God telling us that Judas was an evil, self-centered cheat, and we have you telling us that he thought Jesus was the Messiah? So what we have here is your word against the word of God, isn't that correct?

FRIEND OF JUDAS

I am not a liar!

ATTORNEY JUSTICE

When Judas allegedly told you that Jesus was the Messiah, did you believe him?

FRIEND OF JUDAS

Yes, I did.

ATTORNEY JUSTICE

You believed Jesus was the Messiah, too?

FRIEND OF JUDAS

Yes, I tell you!

ATTORNEY JUSTICE

Then why didn't *you* follow Jesus?
Pause
I think you're lying to this Court, Friend of Judas!

FRIEND OF JUDAS

I am not lying!

ATTORNEY JUSTICE

If Judas told you that Jesus was the Messiah and you believed him, then why didn't *you* go with Judas that night to arrest him?

FRIEND OF JUDAS
Well ...

ATTORNEY JUSTICE
Why weren't you there to see the fireworks if you and Judas thought Jesus would come into his power?

FRIEND OF JUDAS
I ... I ...

ATTORNEY JUSTICE
We have your word against the word of God, right? You tell this Court one thing and the Bible says something different. No more questions, your Honor.
Takes seat

JUDGE
Mr./Ms. Grace? Care to redirect?

ATTORNEY GRACE
No, your Honor.

JUDGE
Very well. The witness may step down.
FRIEND OF JUDAS exits.
Mr./Ms. Grace, the Defense's next witness?

ATTORNEY GRACE
Crosses to examination stand
Your Honor, if it pleases the Court, the Defense calls a Chief Priest to the witness stand.

The "oath" takes place in front of the Judge's bench; BAILIFF and CHIEF PRIEST cross to the front of the Judge's bench, and they face each other.

BAILIFF

Please raise your right hand ...
BAILIFF raises hand also.
Do you solemnly swear to tell the truth?

CHIEF PRIEST

I do.
BAILIFF crosses to his seat, and CHIEF PRIEST crosses to the witness stand for questioning.

ATTORNEY GRACE

Were you a chief priest at the time of Jesus' death?

CHIEF PRIEST

Yes. We had one high priest, 24 priestly families — of which I, as a chief priest, was a part — and several Levitical priests.

ATTORNEY GRACE

How did you become a chief priest?

CHIEF PRIEST

One had to be born in the family of Aaron. And I had to be free from any physical defects. We were the custodians of the sacred tradition, and we had the authority *par excellence* in all matters relating to the law of Moses.

ATTORNEY GRACE

As the custodian of the sacred tradition, did you and the other chief priests want to kill Jesus?

CHIEF PRIEST

Jesus was a problem for us. His teachings were not always in line with the law. And too many people were following his teachings. Yes. Jesus was a threat to the law. He had to be dealt with.

ATTORNEY GRACE

When did you and the others first seek to destroy Jesus?

CHIEF PRIEST

When word came to us that Jesus had raised Lazarus from the dead. We thought it was a bunch of hocus-pocus, another reason to do away with him.

ATTORNEY GRACE

Were you happy when Judas came to you with a proposal to betray Jesus?

CHIEF PRIEST

Smiling
Most definitely. I offered him thirty pieces of silver.

ATTORNEY GRACE

How much would that be for us today?

CHIEF PRIEST

About $10,000.

ATTORNEY GRACE

My! You really did want to get rid of Jesus, didn't you? Did Judas say *why* he was doing this?

CHIEF PRIEST

We were curious about that. After all, he was a follower of Jesus. But Judas didn't say much. We really didn't care, so long as we got Jesus.

ATTORNEY GRACE

After Judas handed him over to you, what did Judas say?

CHIEF PRIEST

Judas returned to the Temple with the money. He threw the money across the floor. He said, "Take your money back! I have betrayed innocent blood."

ATTORNEY GRACE
Then what happened?

CHIEF PRIEST
He ran away. Later we discovered that he killed himself.

ATTORNEY GRACE
So was Judas sorry for what he had done to Jesus?

CHIEF PRIEST
It sounded like that to me. But giving the money back was not going to solve his dilemma.

ATTORNEY GRACE
Thank you, Chief Priest. No more questions, your Honor.
Takes seat

JUDGE
Your witness, Mr./Ms. Justice.

ATTORNEY JUSTICE
Crosses to examination stand
Sir, for the Court, describe how Judas reacted when you offered him $10,000 to betray Jesus.

CHIEF PRIEST
He seemed pleased. Almost anxious. He demanded the money up front.

ATTORNEY JUSTICE
Now, when he came back and threw the money on the Temple floor, did you put the money back in the Temple treasury?

CHIEF PRIEST
Absolutely not! It was blood money! It was unclean.

ATTORNEY JUSTICE
What do you mean by "unclean"?

CHIEF PRIEST
It was money defiled by greed and evil purposes. We could not put it back in the treasury. So we bought a field with it to bury poor people.

ATTORNEY JUSTICE
One final question. Are you familiar with the Scripture that reads, "If someone sins against another, someone else can intercede for the sinner with the Lord. But if someone sins against the Lord, who can make intercession?"

CHIEF PRIEST
Yes. That was delivered to Eli the priest for the sins of his sons against the Lord in the Temple.

ATTORNEY JUSTICE
Did it call upon the wrath of the Lord?

CHIEF PRIEST
With a vengeance.

ATTORNEY JUSTICE
Thank you, Chief Priest. No more questions, your Honor.
Takes seat

JUDGE
The witness may step down.
CHIEF PRIEST exits.
Mr./Ms. Grace, your next witness.

ATTORNEY GRACE
Crosses to examination stand
Your Honor, if it pleases the Court, the Defense recalls the disciple Peter as an adverse witness.

PETER crosses to the witness stand.

JUDGE
Peter, I remind you that you are still under oath.

PETER
Yes, your Honor.

ATTORNEY GRACE
Peter, would you say that the traditional Jewish view of the Messiah was that God would come in a show of power and destroy all of the enemies of Israel and then set up Jerusalem as God's throne?

PETER
Yes. That was the traditional view. But Jesus told us that he must suffer and die.

ATTORNEY GRACE
Did you believe that Jesus was the Messiah?

PETER
Yes, I did. At one time in our ministry Jesus asked us who we thought he was. I said that he was the Messiah, the Son of the Living God.

ATTORNEY GRACE
According to Scripture, after you made that wonderful confession, then Jesus started talking about how he must suffer and die. Is that true?

PETER
Yes.

ATTORNEY GRACE
But you didn't believe him, did you? You said that he would not die, isn't that true?

PETER

I guess I didn't want to face it.

ATTORNEY GRACE

Or is it because *you* also believed the traditional view of the Messiah? Peter, you really didn't think Jesus could die, did you?

ATTORNEY JUSTICE

Objection, your Honor. Counsel has been leading the witness for quite some time.

JUDGE

Counselors approach the bench.
ATTORNEY JUSTICE and ATTORNEY GRACE cross to bench, converse with JUDGE, and cross back to their seats.

JUDGE

Since Peter was called as an adverse witness, Mr./Ms. Grace is allowed to ask leading questions. Therefore, I overrule the objection. Continue, Mr./Ms. Grace.

ATTORNEY GRACE

Thank you, your Honor. When Jesus was teaching about suffering, rejection, and death, isn't it true that you rebuked Jesus?

PETER

Yes.

ATTORNEY GRACE

How did Jesus respond to you?

PETER

He said, "Get behind me, Satan."

ATTORNEY GRACE

You mean Jesus called you Satan, the devil?

PETER

Yes. But in my case he was joshing.

ATTORNEY GRACE

Oh, really? "Get behind me, Satan," said Jesus, "for you are not setting your mind on divine things but on human things." Does that sound like a joke to you?

PETER

No. I guess you had to be there.

ATTORNEY GRACE

The fact is that Judas is not the only one who was called a devil. You earned that title, too, didn't you?
PETER does not answer.
Let's switch to the Last Supper. You previously testified that Jesus took a loaf of bread and a cup of wine and said that they were his body and blood, given and shed for you. Did Jesus tell you why he was doing this?

PETER

The Passover celebrates the salvation of God's people from bondage. Originally, lambs were slaughtered and their blood was placed over the doorposts of the Hebrews to protect them from the angel of death.

Jesus was the true Passover lamb, sacrificed for our sins, sparing us from death. So that night at the Passover meal, Jesus said, "This is my blood of the New Covenant, shed for you for the forgiveness of sins."

ATTORNEY GRACE

For the forgiveness of sins! Did Judas partake of the body and blood of Christ that night given for the forgiveness of sins?
Pause

PETER

Yes, he did.

ATTORNEY GRACE

So Judas did share in the Lord's Supper — in the forgiveness of sins! Thank you, Peter. No more questions.
Takes seat

JUDGE

Mr./Ms. Justice, the Prosecution may cross-examine.

ATTORNEY JUSTICE

Crosses to examination stand
Now, a lot of testimony has been presented on both sides about whether or not Judas actually believed Jesus was the Messiah. In the Garden of Gethsemane that night, who led the crowd to arrest Jesus?

PETER

Judas. He was right there in front.

ATTORNEY JUSTICE

What, if anything, did Judas do?

PETER

He hypocritically identified Jesus with a kiss. Then the soldiers swarmed on Jesus.

ATTORNEY JUSTICE

What, if anything, did Judas say after they seized Jesus?

PETER

Judas yelled, "Better take him under guard!"

ATTORNEY JUSTICE

Take Jesus under guard?

PETER

Yes.

ATTORNEY JUSTICE

And you heard Judas say that?

PETER

As plain as day. Because that's when they bound his hands, and Jesus said, "I've been in the Temple many times. Why do you take me by force in the dark of the night?"

ATTORNEY JUSTICE

Peter, help me out. Is there any reason why a person who believed Jesus is the Messiah would want him taken *by force under guard*?

PETER

I have no idea. It makes no sense to me.

ATTORNEY JUSTICE

It doesn't to me either. Thank you, Peter. No more questions, your Honor.
Takes seat

JUDGE

Peter, you may step down.
PETER exits.
Mr./Ms. Grace, I understand that you have two final witnesses for your case?

ATTORNEY GRACE

Yes, your Honor. The Defense is having difficulty locating one of the witnesses. With the Court's permission, we call for an extension.

JUDGE

So granted. This court is in recess until next Wednesday night at 7:00 p.m. At that time I will expect both sides to present their closing arguments, and we will poll the jury.
JUDGE hits gavel and exits.

BAILIFF

All rise.

After JUDGE exits, say:

You may be seated. Let us continue our worship by presenting our gifts to the Lord.

Lenten Service

Act V
Who Will Save Us?

CONFESSION: Psalm 51:9-15 (NRSV)
L: Hide your face from my sins,
C: And blot out all my iniquities.
L: Create in me a clean heart, O God,
C: And put a new and right spirit within me.
L: Do not cast me away from your presence,
C: And do not take your Holy Spirit from me.
L: Restore to me the joy of your salvation,
C: And sustain in me a willing spirit.
L: Then I will teach transgressors your ways,
C: And sinners will return to you.
L: Deliver me from death[1], O God, O God of my salvation,
C: And my tongue will sing aloud of your deliverance.
L: O Lord, open my lips,
C: And my mouth will declare your praise.

CANTICLE	*The Agnus Dei*
PRAYER OF THE DAY	
FIRST READING	Romans 7:14-15, 21-25
GOSPEL READING	Luke 23:26-34a
HYMN	
DRAMA	*Closing arguments follow the testimony of the Apostle Paul and a surprise witness*
OFFERING	
OFFERTORY	
PRAYER	
LORD'S PRAYER	
BENEDICTION	
HYMN	

1. *or* bloodshed

93

Act V

Who Will Save Us?

BAILIFF enters.
BAILIFF
All rise.
Loudly and quickly as JUDGE enters
Hear ye, hear ye: The Lenten District Court of _____
_____ Church is now in session, the Honorable Judge I. M.
Pilate presiding.

JUDGE

JUDGE sits.
You may be seated.
BAILIFF takes his seat near the bench.
Mr./Ms. Grace, is the Defense prepared to complete its case to-
night?

ATTORNEY GRACE
Yes, your Honor. We have two final witnesses.

JUDGE
Very well. Then we'll have closing arguments and poll the jury
for a verdict — tonight — unless the Prosecution objects.

ATTORNEY JUSTICE
Not at all, your Honor. The Prosecution would welcome closing
arguments tonight.

JUDGE
Good. Mr./Ms. Grace, you may begin with your next witness.

ATTORNEY GRACE
Thank you, your Honor. If it pleases the Court, the Defense calls
its next witness: the Apostle Paul.

The "oath" takes place in front of the Judge's bench; BAILIFF and APOSTLE PAUL cross to the front of the Judge's bench, and they face each other; ATTORNEY GRACE crosses to the examination stand.

BAILIFF

Raises right hand
Please raise your right hand. Do you solemnly swear to tell the truth?

PAUL

I do.
PAUL takes seat at the witness stand; BAILIFF returns to his seat.

ATTORNEY GRACE

Saint Paul, welcome to our century. For the record, would you tell us about yourself?

PAUL

Certainly. I was a first-century Jew. I was born at Tarsus and given the name "Saul." I was a Pharisee from the tribe of Benjamin, and by trade I was a leather-worker.

At one time in my life, I persecuted every Christian I could find. I even had a hand in the death of Stephen, who was the Church's first martyr.

ATTORNEY GRACE

In fact, the Bible says, does it not, that you were known to "breathe threats and murder against the disciples of the Lord."

PAUL

That is most certainly true. I was very zealous for God's law, heavily grounded in Judaism. And I saw Christians as a threat to its existence. Of course, that was before my conversion in the presence of Christ Jesus.

ATTORNEY GRACE

Isn't it true that after your conversion, you became known as "Paul," and you began your ministry for the Lord?

PAUL

Yes.

ATTORNEY GRACE

And isn't it true that you founded churches in Asia Minor and in Greece, and that many of your letters to these churches are included in the Bible?

PAUL

Yes. I was considered a pioneer, because I was the first to formulate and write down the doctrines of the gospel. I wanted to help God's people understand.

ATTORNEY GRACE

What did you want them to understand?

PAUL

I wanted to help people understand the grace of God, and what God had done for them in Christ Jesus. I preached Christ and him crucified.

ATTORNEY GRACE

Saint Paul, if you were to put the Good News of Jesus Christ in a very concise message, what would that message be? In other words, just what has God done for us in Christ?

PAUL

Well, brevity was never one of my strong points. But I would say this ...

All have sinned and fallen short of the glory of God. But through the cross of Christ, we have forgiveness of our sins. And through his resurrection, we have the hope of eternal life. All this is a gift from God, for by grace we have been saved through faith.

ATTORNEY GRACE

Was the cross of Christ part of God's plan?

PAUL

Yes. The crucifixion of Christ was the fulfillment of Scripture, for it was written, "He was reckoned with transgressors." And again, "He was wounded for our transgressions ... And with his stripes we are healed."

ATTORNEY GRACE

What *other* evidence do we have that the cross was part of God's plan?

PAUL

Jesus himself told his disciples on many occasions that the Scriptures found their fulfilment in him, that he would suffer and die. It was God's plan "for the fullness of time, to unite all things in him...."

ATTORNEY GRACE

Saint Paul, you testified that "all have sinned and fallen short of the glory of God." Are you saying that no one is perfect, including someone as devout as yourself?

PAUL

I was the chief of all sinners! "But while we were still weak, at the right time Christ died for the ungodly."

ATTORNEY GRACE

In fact, you even had a difficult time doing good things, didn't you?

PAUL

Yes. There were times when I didn't understand my own actions, because I did not do the things that I wanted, but I did the very thing I hated. We know that nothing good dwells within us. Our minds can *will* to do right, but we cannot do it. It's *not* a matter of willpower. It's our human sinfulness.

ATTORNEY GRACE
It sounds like Judas Iscariot, doesn't it?

PAUL
I think it speaks for everybody. It's like another law at war with the law of my mind and it makes me captive to the law of sin which dwells in me. And, of course, the wages of sin is death.

ATTORNEY GRACE
Well, that's a very wretched state! Who will rescue us from this body of death?

PAUL
Thanks be to God through Jesus Christ, our Lord — and the riches of his grace!

ATTORNEY GRACE
Is the grace of God strong enough, wide enough, and deep enough to extend even to a wretched man like Judas Iscariot?

PAUL
Yes. Nothing in this whole world can separate us from the love of God in Christ Jesus. Nothing!

ATTORNEY GRACE
But Judas did a very bad thing — he betrayed Jesus. Surely there are some sins that would separate us from God's love, don't you agree?

PAUL
No, I don't agree. "God shows his love for us in that *while we were yet sinners* Christ died for us."

ATTORNEY GRACE
Thank you, Saint Paul. No more questions, your Honor.
Takes seat

JUDGE
Mr./Ms. Justice, your witness.

ATTORNEY JUSTICE
Crosses to examination stand.
Saint Paul, are you familiar with the term "universal salvation"?

PAUL
Yes, I'm familiar with it, although it wasn't a term in my day.

ATTORNEY JUSTICE
What does universal salvation imply?

PAUL
Well, universal salvation is a belief that everyone is saved. Some people believe that when Christ died on the cross, he saved the whole world and everyone in it, regardless of whether or not they have faith.

ATTORNEY JUSTICE
Do you believe in universal salvation, that everyone is saved?

PAUL
No.

ATTORNEY JUSTICE
Why not?

PAUL
I believe that God desires everyone to be saved, but not everyone is saved. We are saved by grace *through* faith in Christ Jesus.

ATTORNEY JUSTICE
In fact, you included the word "faith" 140 times in the letters attributed to you in the Bible. Did Judas have faith in Jesus?

PAUL

I don't know. I never met Judas. I never knew him.

ATTORNEY JUSTICE

Thank you. No more questions, your Honor.
Takes seat

JUDGE

Mr./Ms. Grace? Care to redirect?

ATTORNEY GRACE

No, your Honor.

JUDGE

Very well. The witness may step down.
PAUL exits.
Mr./Ms. Grace, I believe the Defense has one last witness.

ATTORNEY GRACE

Yes, your Honor.

ATTORNEY JUSTICE

Your Honor, the Prosecution adamantly objects to any testimony by this next witness. I respectfully remind the Court that this next witness has no bearing on the case, not to mention that it is highly irregular and threadbare at best!

ATTORNEY GRACE

Your Honor, I admit that it is irregular. But I beg the Court to stand by its pre-trial decision and let this witness come forward. The witness was difficult to locate, and I believe the significance will bear out.

JUDGE

Will the attorneys please approach the bench?
ATTORNEY GRACE and ATTORNEY JUSTICE cross to the bench, converse with JUDGE, and cross back to their seats.

Ladies and Gentlemen of the jury, I have allowed my pre-trial decision to stand. The Defense may call its last witness.

ATTORNEY GRACE
Thank you, your Honor. The Defense calls Death to the witness stand.

The "oath" takes place in front of the Judge's bench; BAILIFF and DEATH cross to the front of the Judge's bench, and they face each other.

BAILIFF
Please raise your right hand ...
BAILIFF raises hand also.
Do you solemnly swear to tell the truth?

DEATH
Nods head "Yes"
BAILIFF crosses to his seat, and DEATH crosses to the witness stand for questioning.

ATTORNEY GRACE
Is it true that death came through sin, "and so death spread to all people because all people sinned"?

DEATH
Nods head "Yes"

ATTORNEY GRACE
So "the wages of sin is death," is it not?

DEATH
Nods head "Yes"

ATTORNEY GRACE
Can any human being escape you?

DEATH

Shakes head "No"

ATTORNEY GRACE

Does Almighty God like you?

DEATH

Shakes head "No"

ATTORNEY GRACE

Why not? Is it because God's intention was for us to live with Him
— and not die?

DEATH

Nods head "Yes"

ATTORNEY GRACE

Isn't it true that God desires us to have "life, and to have it more
abundantly"?
No answer from DEATH
Your Honor, please instruct the witness to answer.

JUDGE

Not me. You tell him!

ATTORNEY GRACE

Is it true that, at one time, you and sin separated us from God?

DEATH

Nods head "Yes"

ATTORNEY GRACE

But things have changed, haven't they?
DEATH gives no answer.
The truth is that Jesus Christ overcame the power of sin and death,
didn't he? How did he do that?
DEATH gives no answer.

May I refresh your memory. Jesus was handed over to you —
something he freely accepted. You wanted Jesus, and you thought
you had him dead to rights, didn't you?

DEATH

Nods head "Yes"

ATTORNEY GRACE

And when they nailed Jesus to the cross, you crept in for the kill,
didn't you? Did you rejoice when Jesus said, "It is finished!" and
breathed his last?

DEATH

Nods head "Yes"

ATTORNEY GRACE

Then when Judas saw what he had done, he was sick with grief and
he said, "I have betrayed innocent blood!" But you were not finished yet, were you? You took the life of Judas Iscariot, too, didn't
you? Isn't it true that you want all of us?

DEATH

Nods head "Yes"

ATTORNEY GRACE

And you took Christ, and you held him for three days. But you
couldn't hold him, could you? Instead, God raised Jesus from the
dead. You lost your grip. And now, you don't even have a grip on
us, do you?

DEATH

Shakes head "No"

ATTORNEY GRACE

"Do you not know that all of us who have been baptized into Christ
Jesus have been baptized into his death?" Do you not know that
"we were buried therefore with him by baptism into death, so that

as Christ was raised from the dead by the glory of the Father, we too might walk in the newness of life"?

DEATH does not answer.

Are you not the last enemy to be destroyed?

DEATH does not answer.

Death! You were swallowed up in victory! O Death! Where is *your* victory? O Death, where is your sting?

DEATH does not answer.

Nothing further, your Honor. The Defense rests.

JUDGE

Your witness, Mr./Ms. Justice.

ATTORNEY JUSTICE

No questions, your Honor.

JUDGE

The witness may step down.

DEATH exits.

The testimony is completed. Mr./Ms. Justice, you may present your closing arguments to the jury.

ATTORNEY JUSTICE

Crosses to the lectern

Ladies and Gentlemen of the jury, in a few moments you will be handed a ballot and the time will come for a decision. Should Judas receive eternal punishment for his action? The Prosecution believes he *should*. According to the law, and the testimony of eyewitnesses, and the Bible, Judas was guilty of an eternal crime.

Consider this: there is no evidence that Judas had any faith in Jesus as the Savior. The Defense would have you naively swallow the absurd notion that Judas believed Jesus was the Messiah and that Judas betrayed him to force Jesus to act. But the testimony has refuted that ludicrous idea in two ways: 1) Judas waited to hand over Jesus until the middle of the night in a quiet garden — when he knew there would be no crowd; and 2) after the guards seized Jesus, Judas warned the soldiers to take him under guard.

This is proof beyond any doubt that Judas did *not* believe Jesus would save the world. He betrayed the Son of God for only one reason — greed. And nowhere does it say that Judas sought forgiveness. Nowhere.

We do not believe in universal salvation. It's true that God *loves* everyone, but not everyone is *saved*. Some people simply do not believe.

Ladies and Gentlemen of the jury: God's law is very clear. God's judgment must prevail, or else anything goes and grace becomes cheap. You must return a verdict of eternal punishment!
ATTORNEY JUSTICE crosses back to attorneys' table, while AT-TORNEY GRACE crosses to the lectern.

ATTORNEY GRACE

Brothers and Sisters of the jury, I think we all know that Judas was not perfect. He was, however, deeply sorry for what he had done. His exact words were, "I have betrayed innocent blood!"

In this trial, the Prosecution — not the Defense — had the burden of proof. The Prosecution has failed to prove its case. The law that Mr./Ms. Justice so proudly states says that the *only* unforgivable sin is "blasphemy of the Holy Spirit." Judas made terrible mistakes — which he regretted woefully — but nowhere did he slander the Holy Spirit.

Yes, Jesus called Judas a devil. Yes, Judas betrayed Jesus. But Jesus also called Peter "Satan." Even Peter denied Jesus.

Throughout this trial, we could not avoid taking a closer examination of ourselves and where we also fall short of the glory of God. I don't think any one of us would want to have a trial like this over our own salvation. When it comes to our own lives, we do not want justice from God. We want mercy.

And mercy is exactly what we receive. The Prosecution tried, but they could not touch God's love. When you look at the cross, ask yourself, "Is there a journey so far, a stain so deep, or a valley of sin so wide that would separate us from the love of God?" No.

Let us thank God that Grace is stronger than our sins. Let us thank God that the Lord destroyed the sting of Death. And let us thank God for the words of Jesus from the Cross: "Father, forgive them, for they know not what they do."

Are these words for Judas? Ask yourself, "Are these words for me?"

Thank you, Brothers and Sisters of the jury.

ATTORNEY GRACE crosses to the attorneys' table.

JUDGE

Bailiff, are the ballots prepared?

BAILIFF

Yes, your Honor. If it pleases the Court, I will hand them over to the ushers to be delivered to the congregational jury.

JUDGE nods in affirmation, BAILIFF gives ballots to usher.

JUDGE

Ladies and Gentlemen of the jury, you have been duly sworn. You have heard the testimony, and now you are to decide the punishment, if any, for the defendant Judas Iscariot. God's law that pertains to this case is based on the words of Jesus in the Gospel of Mark, chapter 3, verses 28 and 29:

> *"Truly I tell you, people will be forgiven for their sins*
> *and whatever blasphemies they utter;*
> *But whoever blasphemes against the Holy Spirit*
> *can never have forgiveness,*
> *but is guilty of an eternal sin...."* (NRSV)

The ballot before you has three choices. Mark only one. A line or two is provided if you choose to comment on your verdict. After you make your decision, please fold it once and drop it in the plate during our regular offering.

One final note: This Court does not presume to hold our decision above God's decision. Instead, you are to consider prayerfully the justice of God's law — exposing our sin — and the extent of God's Grace through faith in Jesus Christ, specifically in the case of Judas Iscariot.

Does everyone have a ballot? Very well. The verdict will be declared in this Sunday's bulletin. This Court is adjourned.
JUDGE hits gavel amd exits.

BAILIFF

All rise.
Waits for JUDGE to exit
You may be seated as we offer our gifts to the Lord.